*I*f y

respon...

the pres...

heart, or

up. Patien... ...ore

...... your part may

help open a closed soul—and once that
happens, love could come spilling out.

Throw out the lifeline,
throw out the lifeline,
Someone is sinking today.
—Edward Smith Ufford

God commanded the ravens,
symbols of cruelty, to feed
Elijah [I Kings 17:4] to
show that cruelty may be
turned to kindness.
—Nahman Bratzlav

18

THE LITTLE BOOKS OF

Virtue

KINDNESS

Kindness

EDITED BY LIN SEXTON

Ariel Books

Andrews and McMeel

Kansas City

Kindness copyright © 1995 by Armand Eisen. All rights reserved. Printed in Hong Kong. No part of this book may be used or reproduced in any manner whatsoever without written permission except in the case of reprints in the context of reviews. For information write Andrews and McMeel, a Universal Press Syndicate Company, 4900 Main Street, Kansas City, Missouri 64112.

ISBN: 0-8362-3120-1

Library of Congress Catalog Card Number: 95-60374

INTRODUCTION

"Wherever there is a
human being there is
a chance for kindness."
—SENECA

$\mathcal{B}$E kind to one another. If all of us
lived by this simple maxim, our world
would be an infinitely better place. Few
of us stop to consider how deeply our
everyday lives are affected by small acts
of kindness. Every time we give a com-
pliment, smile at a stranger, hold open a

door, listen to others, share a joke or a Coke, we are making our world a kinder place.

Kindness isn't limited to small acts, of course. All of us have received and bestowed kindnesses of every magnitude. But it's our day-to-day interactions with people that most determine the quality of our lives. A kind and loving environment in the home, a supportive and courteous atmosphere in the workplace, and an open and accepting attitude in the world at large are vital ingredients for our individual and collective well-being.

Kindness is powerful and transformative. It's a virtue we can choose to exercise or not. The writers, poets, religious leaders, statesmen, and sages (anonymous and known) collected in this book all share in the belief that kindness is the right choice—the *only* choice—if we are to live in a nurturing, loving, and peaceful world.

Let us open up our natures,
throw wide the doors of our
hearts and let in the sunshine
of good will and kindness.

—O. S. MARDEN

THROW a pebble into a pond and watch the ripples it creates. Kindness spreads in a similar fashion. A kind act can be a catalyst. It can reach beyond those directly involved. Who can say how far the ripples from one simple act of kindness may spread?

Paradise is open to
all kind hearts.

—PIERRE JEAN DE BÉRANGER

$\mathcal{K}$INDNESS is learned by repetition. Every time we extend a hand in kindness, we get better at it, find it easier, and enjoy it more. As our ability grows, so, too, does our kindness, leaving a surfeit of joy in its wake. Like gold nuggets in a riverbed, little acts of kindness glitter through life in hundreds of different ways.

Kindness can become
its own motive. We are
made kind by being kind.
—ERIC HOFFER

To be able to practice five things
everywhere under heaven constitutes
perfect virtue. . . . [They are] gravity,
generosity of soul, sincerity,
earnestness, and kindness.

—CONFUCIUS

Man is honored for his wisdom,
loved for his kindness.

—S. COHEN

$\mathcal{B}$EING kind is easier said than done. It pains us when proud or difficult people reject our kindness. They don't seem to understand what kindness is or how to receive it. So we resolve to try again, hoping to teach them to graciously accept a kind act.

Kindness begets kindness.
—SOPHOCLES

If someone listens, or stretches
out a hand, or whispers a kind
word of encouragement,
or attempts to understand a
lonely person, extraordinary
things begin to happen.
—LORETTA GIRZARTIS

If I can stop one Heart from breaking
I shall not live in vain
If I can ease one Life the Aching
Or cool one Pain

Or help one fainting Robin
Unto his Nest again
I shall not live in Vain.

— EMILY DICKINSON

Wherever there is a human being
there is a chance for a kindness.

—SENECA

THE old saw "Kill them with kindness" has an odd ring to it. "Kill" and "kindness" together seem oxymoronic. It is true, however, that kindness can thwart anger and hatred, and in so doing convert an enemy into a friend.

We live very close together. So,
our prime purpose in this life is to
help others. And if you can't help
them, at least don't hurt them.

—DALAI LAMA

Do not keep the alabaster boxes of your love and tenderness sealed up, until your friends are dead. Fill their lives with sweetness. Speak approving, cheering words while their ears can hear them and while their hearts can be thrilled and made happier by them. The kind things you mean to say when they are gone, say them before they go.

—ANONYMOUS

One kind word can warm three
winter months.

—JAPANESE PROVERB

In order to be united we must love
one another; in order to love one
another we must know one another;
in order to know one another we
must meet one another.

—DÉSIRÉ-JOSEPH MERCIER

24

$\mathscr{K}$INDNESS is action, not intention. Perform a kind deed—take a step, make a mark upon a situation in some tangible way. Kindness does not merely talk about what it could do, it simply does what is called for.

A little more kindness and a little
    less creed,
A little more giving and a little
    less greed;
A little more smile and a little
    less frown,
A little less kicking a man when
    he's down;

A little more "we" and a little less "I,"
A little more laugh and a little less cry;
A few more flowers on the pathway
   of life,
And fewer on graves at the end of
   the strife.

—ANONYMOUS

No act of kindness, no matter
how small, is ever wasted.

—AESOP

That best portion of
a good man's life,—
His little, nameless,
unremembered acts
Of kindness.

—WILLIAM WORDSWORTH

Kindness in words creates confidence. Kindness in thinking creates profoundness. Kindness in giving creates love.

—Lao-tzu

*W*HEN a child misbehaves or makes a mistake, it may seem kinder to ignore the deed or overlook the error. This form of kindness, however, is unrewarding. Give your child the lessons he needs now, gently and firmly, for this is the true kindness of a parent. Your "harshness" will not seem so in time.

Recompense injury with justice, and recompense kindness with kindness.

—CONFUCIUS

Happiness, grief, gaiety, sadness, are by nature contagious. Bring your health and your strength to the weak and sickly, and so you will be of use to them. Give them, not your weakness, but your energy, so you will revive and lift them up. Life alone can rekindle life.

—HENRI-FRÉDÉRIC AMIEL

$\mathscr{R}$EMEMBER, the pain of being chosen last for the team, or of not being chosen at all? Remember the names you were called when younger? We can all recount small cruelties from our childhoods, both the ones we suffered and the ones we inflicted. Children can be cruel—but they can also be kind. It is our job as adults to reinforce acts of kindness by not letting them go by unremarked. We must be careful that we not only reprimand the cruel act but also recognize the kind one.

What do we live for, if it
is not to make life less
difficult for each other?

—GEORGE ELIOT

A part of kindness consists in loving people more than they deserve.

—JOSEPH JOUBERT

Never lose a chance of
saying a kind word.

—WILLIAM MAKEPEACE THACKERAY

$\mathscr{A}$CTS of kindness are never forgotten by the receptive heart. At the close of day, just before sleep, it is good to reflect on the kindnesses received during the previous twenty-four hours. These memories will gladden your spirit, and serve as models for your own kindnesses tomorrow.

Little deeds of kindness,
Little words of love,
Help to make earth happy
Like the heaven above.

—JULIA FLETCHER CARNEY

*K*INDNESS is the best medicine for stress. Whether you are the giver or the receiver, the effect is much the same. An exchange of kindness restores our faith in humanity and in ourselves—and, in our hectic and driven world, it serves to remind us of the values we cherish the most.

The human contribution is
the essential ingredient. It is
only in the giving of oneself
to others that we truly live.

—ETHEL PERCY ANDRUS

ONCE in a while we suffer from sensory overload and prefer to sit and watch life go by, as on a movie screen. An occasional day like this may revitalize us, but too many can detach us from the world. To become involved once more, we have only to step outside and lend a hand. Kindness communicates and connects.

DAILY acts of kindness can transform a few adjacent streets into a real neighborhood. In neighborhoods like this, people greet one another, by name or with a smile or with a wave of the hand. They take time out from mowing the lawns or shoveling snow to chat. They respect one another's privacy, and watch out for one another's property. They share fruit from their trees and vegetables from their gardens. They enjoy watching one another's kids grow up. Regardless of location, income, or status, kind neighbors make great neighborhoods.

Kind words can be short and
easy to speak, but their
echoes are truly endless.

—MOTHER TERESA

No man is a true Christian
who does not think constantly of
how he can lift his brother, how he
can assist his friend, how he can
enlighten mankind, how he can
make virtue the rule of conduct in
the circle in which he lives.

—WOODROW WILSON

What you do to others
will bear fruit in you.

—SINGHALESE PROVERB

$\mathcal{Y}$OU ring the doorbell and are greeted by a friend with a tray of cookies in her hand and a smile on her face. She is eager to hear your news—to share in your good fortunes, to commiserate over your setbacks. Kindness and friendship are not equivalent, but neither can survive without the other.

You can always tell a real friend:
when you've made a fool of
yourself he doesn't feel you've
done a permanent job.

—LAURENCE J. PETER

$\mathcal{K}$INDNESS respects the dignity of friends and strangers alike. It alleviates embarrassment for those who show up at the wrong time, dressed for the wrong occasion, carrying the wrong gift. Kindness finds solutions, paves the way, smoothes things over, and always makes an effort to save the day—for everyone.

In this world, you must be a bit too
kind in order to be kind enough.

—PIERRE CARLET
DE CHAMBLAIN DE MARIVAUX

Pleasant words are as a
honeycomb, sweet to the soul,
and health to the bones.

—PROVERBS 16:24

The heart benevolent and kind
The most resembles God.

—ROBERT BURNS

*H*OSPITALITY is the art of sharing your home with kindness and generosity. To the weary traveler or shy guest, a hearty and welcoming atmosphere is almost as sweet as home itself. Shared food and quiet conversation, a warm bed and clean towels—these are the simple kindnesses that your guests will remember long after they have left your home.

Shall we make a new rule of life
from tonight: always to try to be a
little kinder than is necessary.

—SIR JAMES MATTHEW BARRIE

$\mathcal{L}$IKE a lamp in the window, or a beacon in the storm, the kindness of loved ones beckons the traveler home. Small kindnesses await the wanderer by the dozen and each of them says, "This is where you are loved. This is where you belong."

I have learned silence from the talkative, toleration from the intolerant, and kindness from the unkind; yet strange, I am ungrateful to those teachers.

—KAHLIL GIBRAN

$\mathcal{K}$INDNESS is a key that will open any door. Remember this when you are locked in a cell of loneliness and despair. Focus on others and their needs, and your kindness will spring the lock and swing wide the gate.

The ministry of kindness is a ministry which may be achieved by all men, rich and poor, learned and illiterate. Brilliance of mind and capacity for deep thinking have rendered great service to humanity, but by themselves they are impotent to dry a tear or mend a broken heart.

—ANONYMOUS

$\mathcal{K}$INDNESS is unique among currencies. Give it away and your pockets will never be empty. Hoard it and it will disappear. In this case it is better to spend than to save.

You have not lived a perfect day,
even though you have earned your
money, unless you have done
something for someone who will
never be able to repay you.

—RUTH SMELTZER

$\mathcal{S}$OME deeds masquerade as kindness, when their true intent is to manipulate or gain attention. These deeds are drawn from a well other than the well of kindness. True kindness needs no fanfare; it is easily recognized by the recipient.

When kindness has left people,
even for a few moments, we
become afraid of them, as if
their reason had left them.

—WILLA CATHER

Kind words are the music of the world. They have a power which seems to be beyond natural causes, as if they were some angel's song which had lost its way and come on earth.

—FREDERICK WILLIAM FABER

$\mathcal{K}$INDNESS can often be measured by what we don't do. When we avoid saying things that would dishonor another, when we refrain from laughing at someone else's expense, when we refuse to manipulate a situation to our advantage and someone else's loss, then we are acting with kindness. Restraint is often the most unselfish behavior of all, because only we will recognize our successes. It might be wise to remember,

however, that every time we avoid an
unpleasantness, we help to make the
world a kinder place.

All the kindness which a
man puts out into the
world works on the heart
and thoughts of mankind.

—ALBERT SCHWEITZER

Kindness is a language
the deaf can hear and the
dumb can understand.

—ANONYMOUS

Little self-denials, little honesties,
little passing words of sympathy,
little nameless acts of kindness,
little silent victories over favorite
temptations—these are the
silent threads of gold which, when
woven together, gleam out so
brightly in the pattern of
life that God approves.

—FREDERIC WILLIAM FARRAR

$\mathcal{K}$INDNESS concerns itself first with bandaging the hurt knee rather than with finding out why the child was climbing the forbidden tree. Kindness follows the dictates of the heart, which means that love always comes first, discipline second.

WHAT TIME IS IT?

What time is it?
Time to do well,
Time to live better,
Give up that grudge,
Answer that letter,
Speak the kind word to sweeten
    a sorrow,
Do that kind deed you would leave
    'till tomorrow.

    —ANONYMOUS

Wise sayings often fall on barren ground; but a kind word is never thrown away.

—SIR ARTHUR HELPS

The way to make yourself pleasing
to others is to show that you care for
them. . . . The seeds of love can
never grow but under the warm and
genial influence of kind feelings
and affectionate manners.

—WILLIAM WIRT

THE WORLD'S NEED

So many gods, so many creeds,
So many paths that wind and wind,
While just the art of being kind
Is all this sad world needs.

—ELLA WHEELER WILCOX

Nothing is ever lost by courtesy.
It is the cheapest of pleasures,
costs nothing, and conveys much. It
pleases him who gives and receives
and thus, like mercy, is twice blessed.
—ERASTUS WIMAN

$\mathcal{I}$T is easy to be kind to people you love and admire. But we should also reach out to others with kindness: read aloud to the bedridden, cook for the bereaved, walk an extra block to show a stranger the way. Sometimes a smile is all that is needed to ward off disaster. We will never know all the ramifications of an act of kindness, but if we reflect for a moment on the kindnesses others have bestowed on us, we can begin to understand the catalytic nature of kindness.

Make a rule, and pray to God to help you to keep it, never, if possible, to lie down at night without being able to say: "I have made one human being at least a little wiser, or a little happier, or at least a little better this day."

—CHARLES KINGSLEY

$\mathscr{B}$E kind. It's good for the soul.

The text of this book was set in
Centaur, and the display in Zipper.

Book design and typesetting by
SARA E. STEMEN